Contents

Preface

There are certain basic principles which we, as practising teachers, have come to value. This book has been written in the hope that it will help Key Stage 2 teachers who share those beliefs, to implement them in their own practice.

The book gives a variety of ideas and is intended for both the specialist and non-specialist. There are a number of ways teachers may use the ideas. Firstly, the teacher may use a single unit for a single lesson. Secondly, each unit has the potential to be developed in greater depth to form the basis of a series of lessons. Finally, the book can provide a number of starting points which teachers may take forward in their own ways.

Each theme contains 5 units and each unit has a structure consisting of:

- Exploring the ideas.
- Making the dance.
- Sharing the work.
- Possible developments.

A variety of teaching and learning styles have been used to enable both teacher and pupils to be fully involved, such as one in which the lesson is largely teacher directed to others in which pupils are given the initial stimulus and are asked to develop it as they choose. We have done this in the hope that readers will share the view that dance teaching requires more than making decisions about the topic of the lesson. Equally important are the teaching and learning strategies employed so that the pupils are fully involved in the work, and learn skills that will serve them both in and beyond the dance context. The drawings are taken from work done by the authors with young people on the particular Unit to which they refer. They are included to illustrate for teachers some of the many ways in which the tasks could be interpreted. A glossary has been included to clarify some of the terms in the book.

We hope that the book will offer some different approaches for teachers and generate some new ideas for the future.

Anne Allen and Janis Coley
Surrey
December 1994

DANCE for ALL 2

Anne Allen and Janis Coley

David Fulton Publishers Ltd
London
Published in association with the Roehampton Institute

David Fulton Publishers Ltd
2 Barbon Close, London WC1N 3JX

First published in Great Britain by
David Fulton Publishers 1995

Note: The right of Anne Allen and Janis Coley to be identified as
the authors of this work has been asserted by them in accordance
with the Copyright, Designs and Patents Act 1988.

Copyright © Anne Allen and Janis Coley

British Library Cataloguing in Publication Data

A catalogue record for this book is available from the British Library.

ISBN 1–85346–369–8

Typeset by RP Typesetters Ltd, 21 Wren Street, London WC1X 0HF
Printed in Great Britain by Bell & Bain Ltd., Glasgow

The Value of Dance in Education

The subject is essential for the personal development of each individual because it is the only one in which the mind, body and senses are fully integrated and share equal roles. Dance has always been used to express people's views of the world. Since an accepted aim of education is the transmission of what is valued in the culture, the worth of dance in our society needs to be considered. It can be spontaneous and social, and every generation re-makes its own dance style.

We believe:

● Dance contributes to the pupil's personal growth, developing the mind, body and senses in a unique combination.

● All pupils have a right to a dance education, where the content and the ways of teaching are appropriate to their needs.

● Children should feel that the work is their own, and have the freedom to experiment within the structured environment of the dance lesson.

● Learning about dance consists of learning to make dances, perform and appreciate them.

Movement is our first language because it can express our thoughts and feelings, making it an important way of communicating. From the first movements of a new-born child to the intricacies of non-verbal communication, movement is a part of all us. It is also the vehicle for dance as a complex art-form.

Through our experiences, interacting with our surroundings, we acquire a 'cultural rucksack' which also influences our art. This in turn affects others we interact with. Education in dance aims to develop the skills, sensitivity and perception through which this continuous transaction takes place.

Physical skills (both fine and gross), control and co-ordination, flexibility, stamina and strength, are important to dance. Additionally, dancers learn to develop their sixth sense, the kinaesthetic, by increasing their awareness of what the body is doing, where and how it is moving. All learning initially takes place through the senses: the baby explores its immediate world through touch, taste etc. Through sensory perceptions, the body is the point of reference for our interaction with our environment. The dancer 'makes sense' of what is happening through the kinaesthetic, tactile, visual and auditory messages received.

As feelings are registered through the senses, so education of the senses will result in a greater awareness of the ways in which movement can be expressive. The development of this ability is crucial to children's artistic and aesthetic education, whether in the role of choreographer, performer or observer.

Just as the senses and feelings function in an integrated way with the body, the mind is also interdependent. For example, the understanding of concepts and the ability to

v

recall are central to learning and also allow the dancer to visualise, reflect, interpret, imagine and create.

In addition to what is learned through the mind and body, children also learn to work with others. The dance lesson requires pupils to share the working space and at times to work with others in making and performing dances. Another kind of social interaction happens as we learn about different dance forms. This can help us to appreciate the contexts of the dance including the people who have initiated and developed them. Understanding the origins of the dance culture will enrich the child's experience and therefore contribute to the learning process.

The importance of dance in education is therefore multi-faceted. Its richness lies not only in how it develops the individual, but in the ways it can also contribute to children's social and cultural education.

Learning in Dance

For pupils, the dance lesson is primarily experiential. However learning in dance is more than only taking part in a physical activity. The opportunity to create their own dances is important for children and also learning to observe and reflect on their own work and that of others. Young people should be given the chance to develop the skills of choreographing, performing and appreciating. This three-stranded approach is an established model for teaching dance and has been used throughout this book. It is also present in the National Curriculum, through the statutory Attainment Target.

The three strands may be taught simultaneously; for example, pupils from an early age can make critical comments about dances as well as being able to make dances and perform them. Additionally, each strand makes certain demands on children.

Choreographing is the process of putting together movements with the ultimate aim of producing whole dances. On a basic level it involves making choices about movements. From the simplest decisions children make about their own actions, for example whether to jump on one or two feet, to pupils developing a group dance for performance, the demands remain essentially the same. Fundamental decisions must be made about such things as the actions and movement qualities to use and, perhaps more complexly, where and when the dancers will move in relation to each other and to the performance space. Children are learning how to create a unified whole appropriate to the stimulus they have been given.

The role of the teacher is to help pupils to develop a number of skills such as experimenting with ideas, analysing them and selecting the most suitable. It is important to allow time for pupils to work through these stages and for them to use their imagination in seeking innovative solutions to the task.

The interpersonal skills are equally important. Often in lessons, pupils will be working with others to make dances and young people need to learn the skills of listening, negotiating and perhaps compromising before decisions are reached. On other occasions, one person may be given responsibility for all or part of the decision-making and it will be dependent on others to co-operate.

The performance strand may consist of pupils presenting dance choreographed by others or their own compositions. It could be to realise their planning in practice or setting out to present to a specific audience, albeit fellow class members. Performance skills include the basic actions of jumping, turning, balancing, taking and giving weight, and movement qualities such as the flow of energy and changes of speed. The teacher needs to provide challenges for pupils to improve the quality of their movements as they dance, the way they control their movements and an awareness of the dance space itself. Learning the skills of presentation such as expression, clarity, projection and commitment must also be practised. Mastering these skills can improve self-image and increase confidence as the pupils become more competent, through encouragement and frequent opportunities, to present their work to others.

The third strand of appreciating requires the development of judgement and the ability to interpret dance, and it is possibly the most important strand as it permeates through the other two. Skilled dancers will constantly reflect on their work as they perform and adapt it accordingly. It is this ability which enables dancers to improve their performance by making it more accurate, more fluent and more manageable. It may also allow the creator to perceive the work as the audience might see it. Above all, this strand aims to foster an appreciation of quality by the pupil.

The first stage in the implementation of this strand is the development of observation skills, when children learn to look at specific aspects of a dance. This may be their own dance, other class members' work or movements shown by the teacher or on video. A simple viewing task, such as noticing and identifying one class member who has involved the whole body in the movement, is a start in helping pupils focus their attention on particular points which make good performance. The next stage is to learn to describe what is seen, for example, through comments such as, 'Those dancers are swinging their arms as they jump.' Later, comparisons can be made and pupils asked, 'Which dancer is making the widest shape?' Through these observational practices pupils will gain a sense of what are considered to be good points and will support the stage of making independent value judgements and explaining these by giving examples from their own perceptions. As pupils become more expert in the skill of appreciating, so they will be able to distinguish between a variety of dance forms as well as different levels of performance.

It is important that pupils feel free to make their own decisions and are not hampered by anticipating what the teacher expects them to say. If the climate of the lesson is supportive, that is if pupils feel free to speak, knowing that their views will be heard and respected, then they will gain confidence in their own judgements and this in turn will support their efforts at being creative. Evaluating dance is not a simple or passive process of observation and in the last resort, pupils will place an interpretation on the dance as a result of their own experience and perceptions. Such full and active involvement in the lesson is an important factor in developing pupils' capacity to evaluate in dance.

Glossary

The glossary offers an explanation of some of the terms used in the book as we explain **WHAT** dance actions are, **HOW** the body moves, **WHERE** the dancers moves to, the **RELATIONSHIPS** which have to be considered and **WHY** this particular dance is being made.

WHAT

●*PARTS OF THE BODY* – The body can be moved as a whole or certain parts can be emphasised.
Example: the elbow leads the action.

●*BODY DESIGN* – The way the dancer chooses to shape the body in movement or stillness.
Examples: angular, extended, wide, twisted, symmetrical.

●*TRAVEL* – Moving into another part of the space on any part(s) of the body.
Examples: walk, run, roll, crawl, slide.

●*GESTURE* – Actions where part or all of the body bends, stretches or twists, without travelling.
Examples: reach, contract, coil, rise, fall, open, close.

●*STILLNESS* – Where the body is actively held stationary.
Examples: freeze, pause, hesitate, halt.

●*JUMP* – The whole body takes off from the floor.
Examples: hop, spring, leap, bounce and variations.

●*TURN* – Actions which cause the whole body to face a different direction.
Examples: spin, spiral, whirl, wind.

Combinations of these actions – for example, gesturing whilst jumping and any variations – form the fabric of dance.

HOW

How the body moves will begin to give the movement particular qualities, sometimes referred to as 'dynamics'. The quality is what makes the movement expressive.

●*TIME* – Pace, changes of speed, rhythm and phrasing.
Examples: lingering, dashing, sauntering, slowing, accelerating, regular.

●*ENERGY* – Different degrees of body tension or power.
Examples: floppy, forceful, strong, heavy, relaxed, light.

●*FLOW* – Whether the action is performed freely and continuously or in a more hesistant, contained way.

WHERE

All the ways in which the dancer uses the space.

●*LEVELS*
Examples: high, low, in the middle space.

●*DIRECTIONS.*
Examples: forwards, backwards, sideways.

●*PATHWAYS* – These can be on the floor or the pathways which the movement traces in the air.
Examples: travelling along zig-zag, tracing a circle in the air.

RELATIONSHIP

The relationship may be between parts of the body, the dancer and an object or one or more dancers.

●Relationships with the partner(s) will be established by factors such as how they oreintate and how close they are to each other, with or without contact.
Examples: near to/far from, facing, back to back, above and below, matching and contrasting.

WHY

The dance will be shaped by the dancer's intentions. How (s)he moves will be influenced by the attitude and what the dance is about, which may be to communicate an idea, or purely for the sensation of enjoying moving in space.

Theme 1   **The Body**

1.1   The Skeleton

The dance explores ways in which the joints can move, introduces ideas about isolating or focusing on certain movements and taps into the humorours ideas which children have about skeletons.

Resources

1. Pictures or articulated models of the skeleton.

2. Poems about skeletons.

3. Music: Dry Bones'. *Rain Man* soundtrack. Capitol C4 91866

Exploring the ideas

Establish that children understand about joints, and can name some.

1 Using one joint, find out how many ways you can move it, e.g. the shoulder can move forwards/backwards, up/down and round.

2 Experiment with other joints, find still positions that draw attention to that part of the body, that make it noticed.

Teaching point
This attention may be achieved through focusing on it, holding that part of the body away from the rest, or making contact with it.

3 Try out ways of travelling, making sure that the chosen joint action leads the movement.

Teaching point
For example – tell pupils to let that part of the body pull them suddenly to another part of the room or to make a clapping action with the knees which develops into a walking action.

4 Explore actions on the spot, with the joint leading, e.g. the elbow.

Teaching point
Encourage clarity of movement, ask pupils to decide in which direction the action moves and how is the rest of the body helping?

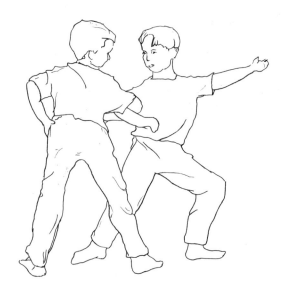

'Shaking hands' with different parts of the body

Making the dance

① Begin close to the floor, in a position chosen from ideas in ② above. Use your ideas from ③ above to rise. Travel as for ④ above around the room.

② Meet a partner. Try 'shaking hands' but with different parts of the body. Have a movement conversation (one move at a time) emphasising the part of your body you have chosen.

Teaching points:
(a) Encourage pupils to use the whole of the body, led by one part.
(b) One dancer stays still whilst your partner is moving.
(c) Suggest to pupils that they 'dance loudly' by jumping and turning to give emphasis.
(d) Praise original or humorous exchanges.

Sharing the work

Several pairs demonstrate at a time.

Teaching point
*Observers look for and comment **either** on dances where it is clear which part of the body is leading **or** on partner dances where the conversation is expressive.*

Possible developments

Get into groups according to the joints you have chosen, i.e. all the 'knees' work together. Develop a dance including the three elements above e.g. stillness, travelling and actions on the spot.

The teacher's own notes

1.2 The Blood

Starting with the words which the pupils provide in a brain-storm to describe the ways in which the blood moves – e.g. flowing, rushing, spurting, clotting – the dance explores these as movement ideas.

Resources

Music: 'Yes Pulstar'. *The Best of Vangelis.* RCA PK 7011

Exploring the ideas

CIRCULATING – Section 1

1. Fast running, in and out of each other, using whole space.

Teaching points
(a) Pupils should cover as much of the space as possible, watching out for others.
(b) Remind pupils to run lightly.

2. Repeat travelling but this time slowly, using different parts of the body, for example sliding, rolling.

Teaching point
Suggest that pupils move as if in a slow-motion film, keeping the movements smooth.

3. Travel fast and then change to slow when given signals.

Teaching point
Pupils should work at accelerating and decelerating gradually and smoothly.

4. With a partner, one makes a shape which the other can move **over, round, through** and **under.** Change over so that you can both try.

Teaching point
Partners should discuss how they can best help each other e.g. stable, varied shapes, moving without touching.

CLOTTING – Section 2

Everyone jogging lightly in whole space, when the teacher calls a number, that number of pupils must instantly make contact and remain in a still position. Repeat with the teacher calling different numbers each time.

Teaching point
Use works like wrapping, clotting, to encourage use of whole body. Varying parts used for contact, not only hands but large body parts too, will increase the range of the work.

Making the dance
CIRCULATING – Section 1

One from each pair becomes A, the other B. A's remain still in their preferred shapes. B's rush in and out, choose when to slow down and begin to move under, over, through and round any of the A's in their path. On a signal from the teacher, B's slow down into a still position and A's become the travelling group.

A's choose when to slow down and finish in contact with one of the B group. The B person moves away and circulates whilst A remains in the same position until contacted by another B. The dance ends when everyone is still, in contact, in twos.

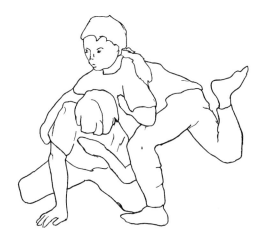

Clotting

Sharing the work

Half the A's together with half the B's demonstrate. Groups change over.

Teaching point
Observers should look for and comment on good contrasts of speed, good co-operation in pair work.

Possible developments

◇ Further section on 'spurting' interepreted through sudden travelling jumps, in a variety of directions.

◇ The clotting section could be extended to form groups of any size or number where pupils have good observation skills and can see possibilities for making contact with more than one other person.

1.3 The Heart

This dance aims to capture the rhythmic pulse of the heart and the power needed to expand, contract and force the blood around the body. It introduces the use of percussion instruments as a form of accompaniment.

Resources

1. Percussion instruments which can produce a short sharp sound are preferable. Pupils can clap or beat feet on floor if there are insufficient instruments.

2. Metronome or keyboard to set tempo.

Exploring the ideas

Body tension exercises

These are used to introduce the pupils to the idea of the power of their muscles (of which the heart is one) in static positions or in movement. Any of the following activities may be used.

☐1 Sitting and hugging yourself tightly, arms wrapped around knees, squeeze the body hard, feel the power of the muscles, release and repeat.

☐2 (As for ☐1) but the teacher tries to undo the 'parcel' by moving your arms or legs, whilst you resist.

Those who resist successfully, may be invited to then help the teacher to 'undo' other 'parcels'.

Teaching point
Safety: Pupils working with others must realise that care of the other person is most important.

☐3 Sitting back to back in pairs, hands and soles of feet flat on floor, on a signal, exert as much force as possible, to push your partner away.

☐4 In twos, one of you lies on the floor, as if glued in place. Partner places hands beneath the shoulder and hip or leg and tries to roll partner over, whilst s/he resists.

Dance task

☐5 Remembering what you experienced in the body tension exercises, work on a pushing action, using the whole body, moving outwards suddenly and forcefully and then pulling back quickly and energetically.

Teaching points
(a) Check that the power is maintained throughout the phrase.

(b) Pupils should use the whole body, particularly the spine, leading with parts other than the arms should be suggested if necessary.

☐6 Using percussion instruments, keeping in time with the rest of the class, play a rhythm of four even beats to the bar.

Teaching point
The teacher should conduct the playing at a speed which will allow the dancers to use two beats to expand, two to contract.

☐7 Repeat ☐6, emphasising the first beat, then the first and third.

Teaching Point
Beat 1 will initiate the pushing action, beat 3 will initiate the pulling action.

8 Return to your pushing and pulling action. The teacher will accompany on percussion. Emphasise beats 1 and 3 by making these movements more powerful.

Teaching point
Encourage pupils to use a variety of levels and directions for example – try with all body parts going out simultaneously into different directions, then the whole body shooting out into one direction and contracting in the opposite one, e.g. upwards/downwards.

Pushing and pulling

Making the dance

In twos, find ways of using the pushing and pulling action simultaneously, working in different pairs of directions – e.g. if A is using upwards/downwards, B could use side to side.

Teaching points
(a) Encourage pupils to to work as closely as is safely possible.
(b) Encourage pupils to make the movement as large as possible by using the feet and legs.

Sharing the work

Half the class demonstrates in its pairs, the remainder accompany on percussion led by teacher and maintaining the rhythm.

Teaching points
(a) Observers should look for dancers showing energy throughout their work.
(b) Percussion players should assist the dancers as much as possible by keeping accurately to the rhythm and the tempo.

Possible developments

◇ Pairs could combine their patterns into larger groups.

◇ A travelling action could be developed from the pushing and pulling area.

◇ Dancers maintain same rhythm but then slow down and speed up to same tempo again.

The teacher's own notes

1.4 The Lungs

Here the movements of expanding and contracting, rising and falling are explored and the intention is to develop awareness of the dancer's own pattern of breathing and the qualities of lightness, ebb and flow and continuity.

Resources

1. Working with a parachute will give pupils the chance to see air lifting, supporting and expanding the fabric, with a flowing, wave-like, action: the dynamics which their dance will try to capture.

2. Balloons. Keeping a balloon in the air with light touches will give the pupils experience of light rising actions.

3. Light soft fabrics will show floating, rising, falling actions.

4. Music: 'Gymnopaedies 3'. *The World of the Piano*. Decca 4332224DWO. 'Albatross'. Fleetwood Mac: *25 Years Selections from the Chain*. WEA 9362 45188 4

(c) SAFETY – Children should avoid forced deep breathing for long periods, as this may cause hyperventilation.

② Take a deep breath, run to another part of the room, lightly and with a feeling of being carried by the air, as you breathe out. Slow down and gradually allow the movement to stop as the breath finishes. After a pause, repeat the whole phrase.

③ On the spot, letting your breathing pattern start the action, lift the body upwards and outwards, expanding lightly with a feeling of being suspended in the air and then sinking back as you breathe out. Let the movements become bigger each time.

Exploring the ideas

Introduce the ideas by getting children to be aware of their own breathing pattern.

① Breathe in deeply and expel air slowly, placing hands on your ribs as if to squeeze all the air out of your body. After a pause, watch a partner. How does their body change as they breathe in and out?

Teaching point
(a) Point out the way in which the chest expands and shrinks, rises and falls.

(b) Breathing is an easy, continuous and flowing series of movements, when the body is at rest.

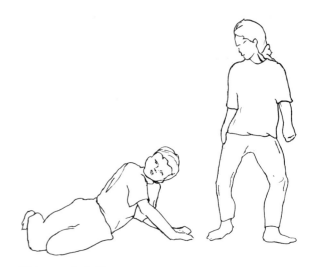

Rising and sinking

Teaching point
Emphasise breathing naturally. Lifting should come from the centre of the body, sinking should be relaxed but not heavy or floppy. The aim is to make the movements continuous, with a sense of ebb and flow, pausing but never stopping.

4 In two's, explore ideas of rising, falling, expanding, and contracting. Select and combine some of the ideas to make a short section, finishing with a still group shape.

Teaching point
Ways of working as a group can include: moving with or without contact, in harmony, alternating (i.e. one rises/expands as the other sinks/contracts), moving towards or away from each other.

Making the dance

Individually, alternate travelling (2 above), with lifting/sinking pattern on the spot (3 above). The third travelling should take you to meet in your groups of four, to perform the expanding/contracting pattern.

Sharing the dance

Class to watch some groups of four at a time.

Teaching point
Class observes for dancers showing uninterrupted light, flowing, actions.

1.5 The Brain

The dance draws not on the scientific views of how the brain works but rather on its capacity for memory and imagination – very important human skills within the creative art of dance!

Resources

1. Paintings by Escher or surrealist paintings.

2. Stories which contain a dream element, e.g. *Alice in Wonderland*.

Exploring the ideas

Introduce the idea of the brain as the centre of our memories, which makes us the individuals we are.

⬚1 Can you remember something from your past and tell a neighbour?

Teaching points
(a) Unusual or interesting memories should be re-told to the class by the listener.

(b) The idea of a listener for each child has the advantage of speeding up the process of telling and giving some confidentiality. (NB: Owner's permission needs to be gained before the memory is re-told.) Secondly, the listener helps to select the interesting or unusual ideas, which also saves time!

⬚2 Take your own memory idea and find a movement phrase to show the whole or part of it.

Teaching point
Initially, pupils will 'act out' their ideas and will need help to translate these into dance. For example, how did you feel at this time? How can you show that? Or, take one action and enlarge it by doing it with the whole body rather than the hand etc.

⬚3 Now consider the brain as the home of our imaginations, which gives us the power to change things. This time, repeat your 'I remember' dance in slow motion, but with a new ending which you invent yourself.

Teaching points
(a) Use the imagery of slow-motion film or video to give pupils the idea of moving in dream-like way.

(b) Encourage imaginative and creative endings, rather than the stereotypical ones.

Making the dance

Find a way of linking the two versions of the dance, choosing which one to begin with.

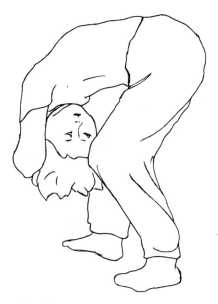

'I remember, I remember . . .'

Teaching points
(a) The finishing position of one version needs to be the same as the start of the second version or a link developed to give continuity.
(b) The dream-like sequence needs to be slow and continuous.

Sharing the work

A number of pupils demonstrate at a time.

Teaching points
(a) The remainder of the class pick out dancers who have achieved a dream-like quality and explain their choices.
(b) Imaginative interpretations of the task and original endings should also be noted and praised!

Possible developments
Nightmares.

The teacher's own notes

Theme 2 The Greeks

2.1 The Circles

The ancient Greeks are remembered today for starting the Olympic Games. The symbol of five linked circles is used at modern Olympics to represent the five continents meeting in peaceful competition.

Resources

An example of the Olympic circles emblem.

Exploring the ideas

1 Explore ways of making different circular air patterns.

Teaching points
(a) Encourage the class to make the circles accurate.

(b) Pupils should try unusual ideas and also to use the whole body.

2 Planes of movement:

● Can you make a circle by moving forwards, high, backwards and then low?

● Can you make a circle that moves forwards, sideways, backwards and to the other side?

● Can you do this at different levels?

Another plane would be to move sideways, upwards, to the other side and then low.

Teaching point
Encourage pupils to use the space above and behind the body particularly.

3 How **large** can you make your circles in the different planes?

Teaching point
Are the pupils using jumps, travelling and turns or spins to extend the circles?

4 Parts of the body.
Consider which parts of the body trace the circle.

Teaching point
Remind pupils to use lower body and trunk as well as limbs.

Making the dance

① Try many different circle ideas and then select three.

Sideways circling

Teaching points
(a) Encourage pupils to choose contrasting ideas. If necessary suggest one or two only of the following, i.e. contrast of planes, levels, body parts leading, travelling or on the post.
(b) Original ideas, which can be well performed should also be encouraged.

② Find a way of linking them together into a short dance phrase.

Teaching point
Pupils should try to use the whole body in their movements and link them together smoothly.

Sharing the work

Perform your completed work to other class members.

Teaching points
Observers should look for and be prepared to comment on dancers who are using the whole body and dances with good use of the contrasts which the teacher set.

Possible developments

Working in threes:
◇ Learn each others' dances and join them together; pupils may have to be prepared to adapt their work.
◇ Find ways of travelling in a circle with your partners.
◇ Each perform your own dance at the same time. Can you adapt it to relate to the others – i.e. can you start or finish at the same time? Do your circles overlap?

2.2 Winning and Losing

The glory and the disappointment of winning and losing are expressed through kinetic sculptures, like Greek statues.

Resources

1. Designs from Greek vases.

2. Photos of winners and losers in modern sports.

3. Music: Opening theme from *Chariots of Fire* soundtrack. Polydor POLDC 5160

Exploring the ideas

Try out different still positions to represent winning. Repeat with ones to represent losing.

Teaching points
(a) Pupils should aim to be completely still, including the eyes.

(b) Facial expression and focus are very important.

(c) Encourage variety of body shapes and levels.

(d) The class should be asked to try to find some shapes and levels which make other parts of the body more important than the arms.

Making the dance

① Select three.

Teaching point
Encourage contrasting body shapes and levels.

② Show your still positions to a partner.

Teaching point
Partner checks for complete stillness and

whether they can identify 'winning' or 'losing' shapes.

③ With your partner, plan the order in which you will both perform your shapes so that they relate to each other's.

Teaching point
Pupils should aim to produce body sculptures with their partners, i.e. need to work fairly close together.

④ Find ways of linking the three shapes by moving very slowly and smoothly from one to another. Make sure that you are both still at the same time.

Teaching point
Emphasise the importance of the stillness.

The glory and the disappointment

Sharing the work

You will all perform your dances, several pairs at a time.

Teaching point:
Ask the class which pairs really look like 'sculptures'? What makes them successful (i.e. they are completely still and show clear focus and design)?

Possible developments

⟨1⟩ Find ways of using the linking movements to move away from and towards your partner.

⟨2⟩ Find ways of rotating during the movement links so that the sculptures face different ways.

⟨3⟩ Adapt your still positions so that there is contact between you and your partner in the still positions.

Teaching point
Different body parts can be used to make contact.

The teacher's own notes

2.3 The Four Elements

The Greeks believed that all matter was composed of earth, fire, water or air. These so-called 'humours' were also thought to define the four main types of temperament and persist to the present day in our astrological 'air' 'fire' 'water' and 'earth' signs of the zodiac.

Resources

1. Examples of horoscopes.
2. List of words describing character.
3. Music: Various tracks from *Fire and Ice*. Torvill and Dean. First Night. CAST C7

Exploring the ideas

Ask pupils to suggest words which describe temperament or personality, e.g. funny, playful, serious, quiet, lively.

Discuss with pupils the ideas that people's temperaments are like the four elements – i.e. fiery, flowing or solid and slow moving.

Which words could be assigned to each category? Which most resembles each individual's nature, in their opinion?

1 *Air* – Travel into a smooth turning jump, and repeat this without stopping, keeping your landings soft, resilient and flowing. Try to let your arms and legs sweep round you as you jump.

Teaching points
(a) The quality of lightness is achieved by lifting through the spine whilst in the air, and keeping an upward focus will also help.

(b) Balance in the air and on landing will be helped by the use of the arms.

(c) Ask pupils if they can change the speed of the action without losing the light flowing quality.

2 *Earth* – Lie as flat as possible, gripping with the body and keeping yourself strong and still as if part of the earth. Rise slowly and strongly and move to place another part of the body in contact with the floor. Repeat this slowly and powerfully so that you travel across the floor, keeping in contact all the time.

Teaching points
(a) Emphasise use of the trunk rather than the limbs to make contact.

(b) Strength can be encouraged if the pupils focus on pulling away from and pressing towards the floor as they travel.

(c) Remind pupils to use lower body and trunk as well as limbs.

Making the dance

① *Air* – After three or four repetitions, let the movement die away and find a finishing position that seems as though you are resting very lightly on the ground and may take off at any moment.

Gripping with the body

Teaching point
Encourage as little contact with the ground as possible.

② *Earth* – During the travelling phrase, slow down and stop when you think your body is in an interesting position and one that shows power.

Teaching point
(a) Ask pupils to check whether they feel the shapes are solid and could not be moved except by tremendous force.

③ Find a way of linking them together into a short dance phrase.

Teaching point
(a) The main contrast should be in the strong/light dynamic and also in the direction of focus e.g. upwards or downwards. Accurate repetition is less important at this stage.

Sharing the work

Perform your completed work to other class members.

Teaching point:
Observers should look for and be prepared to comment on dancers who are using good contrasts of strength and lightness to represent the feeling of being earthbound or airborne.

Possible developments

◇ Add 'Fire' (fast, powerful dynamics) and 'Water' (flowing, weaving).

◇ Group pupils to perform one of the four elements (this could be done according to their 'star' signs).

◇ Allow pupils to choose the element which they consider is most like their own temperament.

2.4 Theseus and the Minotaur

The well-known Greek legend of Theseus and the Minotaur is the starting point for the dance, which is based on depicting the maze and the minotaur (or monster). A spiral is used to represent the maze, as it is fundamental to the Greek key design, and also one of the most ancient dance forms known.

Resources

1. Books of legends/myths.
2. Pictures/paintings/designs including spirals.

Exploring the ideas

The Maze

Establish that pupils understand what a spiral is.

☐ By yourself, walk a spiral pathway, turn and retrace your steps. Make it as large as possible.

Teaching points
Encourage pupils to follow exactly the same pathway when they retrace.

② In groups of eight, join hands, turn to face left, i.e. one behind the other in a chain. As a group follow the leader to walk in a spiral pathway. On reaching centre, leader turns **left** to begin retracing steps, this gradually unwinds the spiral.

Teaching points
(a) Pupils can help each other by keeping even spacing, holding hands lightly and watching each other.

(b) Different leaders should be used.

(c) The leaders will need to be aware of others and prepared to give way.

③ Repeat with whole class forming 'maze'.

The Minotaur

☐ Facing a partner, make the most pleasant face you can, then the most monstrous face possible.

Distorted shapes

18

2 Add distorted shapes with the hands and arms, move the wrists, elbows and shoulders separately.

3 Take a low threatening stance, practise lunging forwards.

4 In fours, discuss your ideas for a group monster shape and find a way of moving together in that shape.

Teaching points
(a) Encourage pupils to listen to everyone's ideas.

(b) Keeping in contact will help.

NB: The minotaur/monster can be a fictitious one, e.g. may have wings, claws, more than four legs, one head.

Making the dance

① Two groups of four link to form the chain and performs the maze dance, moving into and out of the spiral.

② Once again the spiral is completely opened out, each group of four separates and forms into its monster shape. Each group moves in that formation and finishes in a final shape.

Possible developments

◇1 The spiral can be performed using the grapevine step (*see Dance – Greek Style*, page 20).

◇2 Increase number in group.

◇3 Add 'non-human' vocal sounds to accompany the monster formation.

◇4 One of the paired groups develops a unison pattern, on the spot, to represent Theseus wielding his sword.

◇5 Any myth can be taken, parts selected and interpreted through dance, without the necessity to re-tell the story.

2.5 Dance – Greek Style

This dance uses a simple Greek step called the grapevine. It can be taught as a set dance or as the basis for the pupils' own choreography.

Resources

Music: *Never on Sunday* soundtrack. HAT2309 (LP). 'Zorba's Dance' (accelerates) *Zorba the Greek* soundtrack. Silva Screen 825245.4.

Exploring the ideas

NB: The step is taught in the following four stages. Pupils should be competent at each stage before moving on.

1 Start feet together. Step left with the left foot. Close the right foot to the left. Repeat, travelling to left.

Teaching points
(a) Make pupils aware of transferring the weight from one foot to the other.

(b) The right foot touches the left on 'close'.

2 This time, step left with the left foot, cross right foot **in front** of left and step onto it. Repeat, travelling to the left.

Teaching points
(a) The crossing-over the step may cause the hips to turn, but the shoulders should stay facing front if possible.

(b) It will help if both knees are allowed to 'give' in the crossing steps, i.e. kept slightly bent.

3 Start feet together. Step left with left, cross right foot **behind** left and step onto it. Repeat, travelling to left.

4 Complete step. Stand with feet together, step left with left, cross right foot in **front** and step onto it, step left with left foot. Cross right foot **behind** left and step onto it (four steps). Repeat, travelling to left.

Teaching points
(a) Holding the arms out sideways at shoulder level will encourage pupils to keep shoulders facing square, hips can rotate to help crossing over step.

(b) The steps should be kept even, to four regular counts.

(c) Ask for smooth and flowing movements, with only a little rise and fall of the body as the weight is transferred from foot to foot.

The grapevine step

Practise until you are proficient enough to increase the speed (to springy run) and to move in time with one or more partner(s) side by side, with hands joined, then hands resting lightly on each others' shoulders.

Making the dance

① Whole class to perform the steps in one circle, facing centre.

Teaching point
Holding hands helps to establish spacing.

In unison, perform step continuously, travelling to left.

Teaching point
The focus is upwards and outwards, discourage pupils from looking at feet.

② Once the step and timing are established, repeat with hands raised to shoulder height and then resting lightly on neighbours' shoulders.

Teaching point
Check that pupils are keeping shoulders square to centre of circle.

Sharing the work

Both halves of the class demonstrate to the other. Observers look for smooth, flowing steps and whether the group works together as a unit.

Possible developments

◇ Individual pupils experiment with variations on the basic pattern, i.e. changes of direction, changes of level, skipping the pattern etc.

◇ Repeat original step with different arm positions or accompanying gestures.

◇ Make different floor patterns, other than circle.

The teacher's own notes

21

Theme 3 The Environment

3.1 Volcano

This unit will be realised in a group dance representing the ways in which the earth's crust breaks, moves and re-forms.

Resources

1. Video and pictures of volcanoes.
2. Poems about the volcanoes.
3. Descriptive accounts.

Exploring the ideas

The words taken are **spark** and **melt; bubble** and **flow; engulf** and **solidify.**

1 *Spark and melt* — Start near to the floor and spring to land on another part of the floor. As you land, let your body sink very slowly into the floor.

Teaching points
(a) Ask pupils to try to make the body stretched or spiky whilst in the air.
(b) Sink into the floor should be done as if melting. Landing with feet wide apart will help pupils to gain control.

2 *Bubble* — Make the body rounded and jump with your back leading the action, to represent the lava bubbling up.

Teaching point
Partners to check each other that the back is rounded and leads the action.

3 *Flow* – Imagine that the parts of your body touching the floor are firmly fixed there. Pull slowly and strongly against these points of contact and travel by letting other parts of your body sink down and repeat the process. The action should be slow and powerful.

Teaching points
(a) Encourage pupils to use a variety of body parts, including large and small ones.
(b) The pulling action should be slow and even.

Bubbling jumps

4 *Engulf and solidify* – Experiment with moving towards a partner and wrapping yourself around them. Partner moves out and tries the action on you whilst you retain the shape.

Teaching points
(a) Pupils should use a variety of ways of enclosing their partner's shape and different parts of the body to make contact.
(b) The shape should be held unchanged as the partner moves out.
(c) Move as in 3 (lava flow) in between the engulfing action.

Making the dance

① The dance starts with individuals performing 3 of the sparking jumps, and then melting towards the floor.

② The lava flow section follows next, pupils include 3 of the bubbling jumps during this section, when they choose.

③ The dance ends when one pupil (chosen by the teacher) slows into stillness as if solidified and the nearest pupil moves in to engulf him/her. Eventually everyone in the class follows on and a solid lava landscape is formed.

Teaching point
(a) The bubbling jumps should show contrast across the class with the actions of the lava flow.
(b) The process of the whole class solidifying will depend on their co-operation skills, pupils should be encouraged to take unusual but powerful finishing positions, maintaining stillness and contact, to represent the laval landscape.

Sharing the work

Half-class demonstrations.

Teaching point
Other pupils to look for and comment on dancers who show good contrast of dynamics between the light jumps, slow melting, powerful flow and held ending positions.

Possible developments

◇ Pupils suggest other words which might inspire other movement ideas, trembling, hissing, spluttering, smouldering etc.

◇ See unit on *Water*, suggestion for possible development 5 (page 25).

The teacher's own notes

3.2 Water

The changing states of water, vapour, ice and liquid inspire the movements for the dance.

Resources

1. Poems, videos, practical experience with water, in small or large quantities!
2. Music: 'Aldebaran'. Enya. BBC Cassettes ZCF 605.

Exploring the ideas

Water

1 Observe and report on the ways on which water moves. Words such as flow, spiral, pour, splash, swirl etc., can be discussed.

2 Keep one of the words in mind, experiment with ways of travelling, concentrating on keeping the movement continuous, flowing and the body shapes curving. Allow the gestures to develop naturally by involving the whole body in the flowing action.

Teaching points
(a) Emphasise the on-going nature of the movement, and also the changes of level and momentum which will give variety.

(b) Imagining the sensations of being carried and tumbled by water may help.

Steam

1 Use light turning jumps linked with slow smooth travelling across the floor to take off again, for this section.

Teaching point
Emphasise jumps which seem effortless; light, controlled landings, together with curving air and floor patterns.

Ice

1 The movements are crystallised into solid linear shapes with clear body designs. Experiment to find several shapes, at different levels and emphasising different directions. Select your most original and satisfying design.

Teaching point
Changing the points of contact with the floor will give variety.

Making the dance

① Link three sections together, beginning with 'steam' changing to 'water' and ending with 'ice'.

Teaching points
(a) The change of dynamics should be the focus, the movements will be in part improvised, but should be clear none the less.

(b) Signals should be given for the changes in sections.

Sharing the work

Half-class demonstrations.

Teaching point:
*Observers try to pick out dancers who show a change in dynamics **or** achieve one section of the dance with good quality.*

Possible developments

◇ Use of appropriate percussion accompaniment or sound-effects tapes.

◇ The ideas of waves, the water-cycle, rain, etc. can also be explored.

◇ Rain dances from other cultures.

◇ Festivals and rites of passage (such as christening) which involve water could be developed into dances.

◇ The 'water' section could be added to the end of the lava landscape, as the opening two sections on a dance based on the Creation of the Physical Earth.

The teacher's own notes

3.3 Machines

Mechanisation is an important feature of everyday life. Exploring mechanical movements to build group dances is the basis of this unit.

Resources

1. Music: Various tracks from *Best of the Art of Noise*. China WOLMC 1010.
2. Machine parts or picture of them.

Exploring the ideas

Pendulums

Swinging actions. An example should be shown to pupils of a swinging action, e.g. a weighted cord.

⬜ Describe the characteristics, i.e. that the cord does not bend, that the weight gathers and loses momentum, that a shorter cord gives a faster swing, that the pathway is repeated in reverse directions, etc.

⬜ Find which parts of the body can swing, not only limbs, but trunk as well and legs when the body is inverted or in flight.

⬜ Try the same swinging actions around different axes.

Teaching points
(a) Encourage pupils to experience the weight of the body swinging.

(b) Dancers should try to keep the swinging part of the body straight throughout.

Pistons

Explore punching actions which move out from the centre and inwards toward the body. Again, experiment with different ways of carrying this out, using a range of parts of the body, e.g. shoulders, levels and directions.

Teaching points
(a) SAFETY: pupils should work in safe spaces.

(b) The energy should be kept throughout, so that there is an impression of an impulse to begin the movement and an impact to finish.

Making the dance

Make up a solo dance using your ideas for pendulums and then pistons. Repeat each chosen action exactly until the signal to change (i.e. 32 or 64 beats) to pistons.

Teaching point
Each separate action should be repeated exactly and mechanically, although a number of different actions may be chosen.

Pendulum swings

26

Sharing the work

Half-class demonstrations.

Teaching point:
Pupils should look for a robotic and rhythmic dance.

Possible developments

◇① Solos could be grouped and developed to form machines with several working parts.

◇② Other words – such as springs, pulleys, cogs and levers – can be added.

The teacher's own notes

3.4 Re-cycling

The processes of dropping litter, collecting and re-cycling it are the starting points for the dance.

Resources

1. Samples of litter.

2. Samples of paper, metal and play 'slime' for pupils to experience the qualities.

3. Music: Various tracks from *Drummin 'n Dancin 1* or *2*. Primrose Educational Resources.

Exploring the ideas

Discarding the rubbish

1 Discuss the types of rubbish that are dropped, and the actions involved e.g. screwing up paper and throwing it, kicking cans, smashing glass.

2 Choose one action from those discussed and develop an on-the-spot movement to represent it.

Teaching point
Pupils should try to make the movement large and emphatic, for example show the stickiness of the chewing-gum as it is deposited!

3 Choose EITHER a crumpled piece of paper *or* a metal can or a blob of gum and experiment with movements to represent that:

● *Paper* – blows, drifts, flattens, is tossed in the air.

● *Can* – rolls, clatters, is squashed.

● *Gum* – squelches, sticks, smears.

Clearing up

Actions of sweeping, picking up, carrying and heaping together are explored. Select one or two and make a pattern by linking and possibly repeating them.

Re-cycling

In groups to represent moving along a conveyor belt, stand close in a line and shuffle forwards, following a leader. On passing through an area chosen to represent re-cycling, emerge with a new lease of life – run and jump to finish in a position of your own choice to show your new image.

Teaching point
*The class will need to be organised so that they do not all reach the 're-cycling' area at once **or** a sound signal can be given as an alternative.*

Collecting the rubbish

Making the dance

Everyone carries out the rubbish dropping movements, the number of repetitions to be determined by the teacher, and then changes to the actions of the rubbish itself. At a given signal, the whole class performs its 'clearing up' ideas and after a given number of repetitions, moves into conveyor belt formations. Once re-cycled, pupils find a still position until the whole dance is completed.

Teaching point
Using music and set numbers of beats will make the transition smoother if the dancers are sufficiently experienced not to need other cues.

Sharing the work

Half the groups (for the conveyor belt) perform at a time.

Teaching point:
Observers should look for imaginative ways of developing the ideas for 'paper' 'can' or 'gum' to comment on.

Possible developments

◇ Pupils who have experience of contact work could develop the first section by working in twos to carry and release their partners. Safe practice must be a priority.

◇ A machine section could be developed (*see Machines*, page 26), for the conveyor belts to pass through, emerging with a different unison travelling pattern to represent their new image.

The teacher's own notes

29

3.5 The Rain Forest

The destruction of the rain forest and our dependence on the environment are taken as the main themes.

Resources

1. Videos of the rain forests.
2. Music: 'Tropical Dream' or 'Bright Morning' *Tropical Dream*. Holborne SON5 816.

Exploring the ideas

The rain-forest theme is developed in practice through the ideas of counterbalance to show the interdependence of each section of the habitat on another.

1 In twos, sit facing, toes touching and hands linked. Try to rise to standing slowly and smoothly keeping arms extended throughout. Repeat to sit down, with control. Once this is achieved, experiment with the following variations:

● Relesing one hand and extending the arm.

● In standing position turn and lean away from partner.

● Rise and sink at opposite times.

● Combinations of these.

2 Move on now to explore your own ideas for counterbalances.

Teaching points
(a) SAFETY: The task is taught through a closed skill so that it is developed safely. Pupil's own ideas should be developed keeping safety in mind.

(b) Changing the orientation and starting positions will enrich the work.

3 With your partner, experiment to find a unison action to represent the cutting down of the trees.

Teaching point
Stress large movements, whole-body involvement in the action and change of level.

Then work out a way of dropping in a relaxed way to the floor.

Teaching point
SAFETY: Discourage pupils from toppling forward with the body held straight.

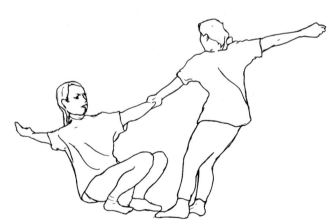

Interdependence

Making the dance

Link together several of your counterbalance ideas, followed immediately by the chopping section, repeated a fixed number of times and end with both of you dropping silently to lie still on the floor.

Because the lengths of the first section will vary, you may find that you will begin and end the destruction section at different times from other pairs.

Teaching points
(a) Encourage pupils to be aware of their partners at all times.
(b) Held still positions at the end will allow others to concentrate on the final parts of their dance. Any pupils who finish too quickly could repeat the counterbalance section twice.

Sharing the work

Half-class demonstrations with partners.

Teaching point
Class members should look for and select pairs who work well together

Possible developments

The work can be choreographed into a whole-class dance, perhaps for performance. For example, the destruction section can be developed so that the chopping action becomes a travelling motif which one pair begins and each pair holds its counterbalance until the leading pair passes. At this point pairs drop and then rise to join in with the same action until the whole class is performing it in unison (there is now no forest left) — and everyone drops simultaneously.

The teacher's own notes

Theme 4 The Explorers

4.1 Hornpipe

A series of set steps and working actions are performed to a hornpipe.

Resources

Music: 'Portsmouth'. *Complete Mike Oldfield.* Virgin CMOCI.
'Blue Peter'. *Complete Mike Oldfield.* Virgin CMOCI.

Exploring the ideas

The dance is based on some simple set steps and working actions.

Skipping

Performed travelling or on the stop, knees turned out and lifted high.

Light running

Performed with the toes pointed, variations of feet stretching either forwards or backwards.

Springs or hops

With the heel of other foot touching the floor slightly to the side. Any variations of these can be included, pupils can invent their own variations. Crossing over the feet, and rocking the weight from one foot to the other.

Try out the above steps and explore ideas of your own.

Teaching points
(a) Light, small steps should be encouraged.
(b) Use the rhythm of the music.
(c) Pupils can travel, in a variety of directions, or move on the spot.

The hornpipe

32

Gestures

Traditional arm positions are:

● Hands behind back, elbows held away from body.

● Arms bent at shoulder height in front of body, with one forearm resting on the other (as if leaning on a wall).

● Pulling on a rope, the heel step gives grip for the pulling action.

● Actions of scrubbing, swabbing decks etc.

● Climbing the rigging – arms alternatively reaching up and pulling down towards the chest.

● Turning a capstan or the ship's wheel.

● Scanning the horizon, with or without a telescope, from the crow's nest.

Teaching points
Working actions should be performed in a lively, energetic way, a good awareness of line, shape and focus.

Making the dance

Since the steps have been taught, pupils are free to concentrate on the formations which the groups will use to perform.

In fours, try out different group formations and pathways.

Teaching points
(a) It may be appropriate to use the device of appointing a group choreographer to listen to the suggestions, but make the final decisions. This experience of being the leader of the team should be given to different pupils at different times.

(b) If pupils have experience of country or folk dance, those patterns may be used.

(c) Pupils can determine the length of their own dance, within reason, or be given a set amount of music.

Sharing the work

Divide the class into three groups. One-third, group A, performs first.

Teaching points
(a) Group B observers look for groups who keep in time and work well together. Group C observers look for groups which have retained the character and identity of the working actions.

(b) The groups rotate tasks to perform and carry out both observation tasks.

Possible developments

◇ Larger groups.

◇ To use some of the steps for a whole-class unison section taught by the teacher or generated by the pupils.

◇ Including patterns based on semaphore.

The teacher's own notes

4.2 Down to Davy Jones' Locker!

Hardships and perils faced by early seafarers, as they crossed uncharted oceans to discover new lands, provide the stimulus for this dance.

Resources

1. Music: Various tracks from Lancashire Bay. Primrose Educational Resources. Sea shanties. Sound-effect cassettes.

2. Accounts of underwater experiences or adventures, either real-life or fictional.

3. Information about life on board sailing ships and the lives of great sailors, e.g. *Treasure Island*.

4. Pictures of ships in sail.

Exploring the ideas

The dance explores the ideas of a large sailing ship, setting out and then being caught in a storm.

☐ *Working actions* – Discuss with pupils the ways in which large sailing ships were powered before mechanisation, e.g. by banks of long oars, or huge sails, raised and lowered by ropes. The effects of a storm at sea on such boats should be explored.

② *The ship begins to roll* – All stand with feet apart, facing the same way and rock from side to side, transferring the weight from one foot to another, as if with the rolling of the boat. This action builds up by enlarging it until it tips you into a controlled overbalance and then you recover to repeat the action.

Teaching point
The aim is to create the effect of being taken by the sway of the boat, and then gradually losing control, but remaining on the feet.

③ *Rushing from side to side* – The next stage is for the movement to build up so that you rush and 'tumble' from side to side of the room. On reaching the edge, hold a still position as if desperately gripping onto something, before being flung back to the other side.

Teaching points
(a) SAFETY: It may be necessary to work half of the class at a time, depending on space, a partner could watch and help each person. If space and co-operation skills allow, pupils can develop this action into a run and slide, so that some of the still positions are held on the floor.

(b) Pupils should be encouraged to explore how to give the effect of being driven from side to side, without actually losing control of their weight.

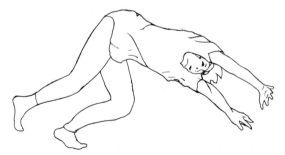
Tipping overboard

4 *Man overboard* – Experiment on the spot with an action of falling, performed in slow motion, to represent the moment of going overboard, the long fall and then sinking down through the water.

Teaching points
(a) SAFETY: The fall is practised and eventually performed in slow motion throughout, letting the knees give in order to relax into the ground.

(b) The facial expression and gestures of reaching out during the falling phase, and adding turning and rising through the sinking phase will give variety.

Making the dance

The class begins in its formation for the 'ship rolls' section, which is performed as a whole-class dance. The actions of sway, overbalance, run and grasp are repeated with the pupils at the front leading the changes of action *or* the teacher giving signals. After doing this three times, everyone holds their final 'clinging on' position until given a signal or cue from the music, to begin the fall overboard movement phase. The dance ends with everyone lying on the floor, with a small, relaxed action of gently swaying from side to side.

Teaching points
(a) The co-ordination of the whole class into one dance could be used for pupils to gain the experience of working in a large group and the observation and co-operation skills needed to do this well. It could also mean that the dance can be used for performance.

(b) The build-up in intensity of the 'ship rolls' section brings the dance to its climax and the slow fall and sinking, with the abrupt change in the dynamics of power and speed will heighten this.

Sharing the work

Half the class, in partners, demonstrate the work.

Teaching point
Pupils look for dancers who manage to change from the powerful, fast rushing and tumbling actions to the slow, weightless descent.

Possible developments

① The dance could begin with a section on working actions, such as rowing or hauling on ropes.

② The unit could be linked to the *Hornpipe* one (page 32).

③ The voyage of the Nautilus, from the book *20,000 Leagues Under the Sea* by Jules Verne, could then be taken as the next stage.

The teacher's own notes

35

4.3 Journey to the End of the Earth

An imaginary adventure presents the traveller with some exciting challenges *en route* to an unknown destination.

Resources

The best resource will be the children's own experience. *See* EXPLORING the IDEAS.

Exploring the ideas

The class discusses the fact that, until 500 years ago, the Earth was thought to be flat and many explorers set out, despite this, to establish where 'the end of the Earth' lay.

Pupils are asked to imagine that they are setting out on a journey, far from civilisation, i.e. without the use of cars, buses, trains etc. Draw on pupils' own experiences of being out of doors, possibly being unsure of their whereabouts, whilst camping, walking, etc.

1 Imagine that you are climbing a very steep hill. Find crawling or hauling actions to pull yourself up.

Teaching point
Ask pupils to use an upwards focus, move in stages, as though picking the route carefully, not necessarily in a straight line.

2 Once at the summit, you stand on tip-toe, arms spread wide to survey the scene before you.

Teaching point
Make a clear link between pulling yourself up to the final point, rising to your feet and stretching with a sense of achievement at having arrived.

3 Running, including rolling and tumbling is the dance phrase for going downhill. This should be worked out, practised slowly at first and then with increasing speed, whilst retaining control.

4 Other possible variations include:
- Crossing stepping-stones.
- Climbing over barriers.
- Squeezing through narrow gaps (imagine caving, pot-holing).
- Struggling through dense undergrowth.
- Wading through deep water, etc.
- Leaping rivers.

At the summit

36

Teaching point
*The teacher should select which and how many of the options are to be used, **or** give pupils a choice. In each case, pupils should first improvise and then practise and learn a short movement phrase for the section, to be linked to the previous one.*

5 The end of the dance is to imagine that you have reached the 'end of the Earth'. What does it look like? What are the features? Are you going on into the unknown or retracing your path? etc. Decide on a way of reacting and a final still position to represent your reactions and the ending you have chosen.

Making the dance

From the phrases you have practised, develop links and a possible order for your solo dance.

Teaching point
The pupils' ability to remember their developed ideas should be stressed.

Sharing the work

Half-class demonstrations.

Teaching point
Which dancers are performing in a way which shows you that they have planned, shaped and practised their work?

Possible developments

◇ A pattern of movements based on the directions of the compass – for example, quarter-, half- and full-turn jumps – could be added as a unison beginning.

◇ The dance could begin with the idea of setting out on a journey. Pupils are asked to imagine that they can only take one precious item. What is it? How will they carry it? The processes of fetching and carrying and packing items could be explored.

◇ Still positions could be introduced with the idea of taking shelter, resting or sleeping at stages on the journey.

The teacher's own notes

4.4 Scott's Footsteps

This unit shows the challenge of travelling across snow and ice in blizzard conditions to the limits of human endurance.

Resources

1. Accounts, both fictional and true, of such explorations.

2. Videos, such as *National Geographic*, of snow-bound terrain.

3. Music: 'Cloudscape'. *Koyaanisquatsi* soundtrack. Island ICM 2036.

Exploring the ideas

Teacher gives background information on Scott's journey to the Antartic.

1 Taking the words **reaching – dragging – sliding**, explore the movement possibilities individually.

Teaching point
Remind pupils to consider which parts of the body are leading the action and taking the weight.

2 In threes, find a way of travelling in contact, to represent the way at times members of the teams had to support each other, in order to keep going.

Teaching points
(a) Words such as leaning, carrying, pulling may help.

(b) Pupils need to consider how the contact is made, which parts of the body are touching or gripping.

(c) Encourage pupils to consider what the group shape looks like. Is there variety of level?

(d) Think of the appropriate speed for the movement.

Making the dance

① Select from ideas explored in the first section and link them.

Teaching points
(a) Pupils need to decide where in the room they will finish this section in order to meet other members of their trio.

(b) Individuals should hold a still position until all the group has arrived.

② Trios travel. Add a still group position to finish the dance.

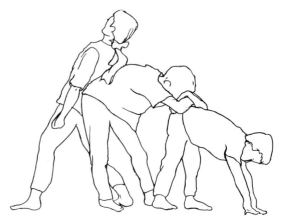

Travelling in contact

Sharing the work

Trios demonstrate a few at a time.

Teaching points
(a) Class observes for good use of contact by the trio.
(b) Which solos show the strenuous effort needed for travelling in difficult terrain?

Possible developments

Add wrapping actions, as if clothing oneself against the cold.

The teacher's own notes

4.5 – The Last Frontier?

The popular topic of space travel captures the imagination of modern would-be explorers.

Resources

1. Videos and accounts, real or fictitious, of space launches and journeys.

2. Music: 'Also Sprach Zarathustra'. *2001: A Space Oddysey* soundtrack. MCA MCAC 39049.

Exploring the ideas

Lift-off

Discuss the amount of power needed to launch a rocket into space.

⊡ Practise single explosive jumps, using as much energy as possible.

Teaching points
(a) Preparing for the jump by bending the knees will help.

(b) Emphasise the need for soft, controlled landings.

(c) Body tension in flight, with linear shapes.

(d) Jumps can be made in different directions to land in new spaces.

⊡ On landing, make a fast curving run on a clear-cut pathway to represent the different trajectories of the rockets.

Teaching point
The pathway should be planned to show that the course has been set and is scientifically pre-determined.

Weightlessness

Explore with the hands the sensations of moving as if being supported on the air and as if they have no weight. Transfer this to moving the arms, shoulders and then upper body. Move on to the feet and travel with large steps, lifting the legs and arms to represent the slow bounding actions of the astronauts.

Teaching point
Travel as if walking on giant marshmallows!

Making the dance

Link the jump and run dance phrases and finish with weightless travelling. Dance ends with a slow-motion tumble as if falling into space.

The launch

Teaching point
Stress the changes in energy/speed dynamics
between the three sections.

Sharing the work

All solos are performed, in groups.

Teaching point
Observers look for contrast in the ways in
which energy and speed are used.

Possible developments

◇ Introduce the dance with a
count-down.

◇ The dance can be extended by
repeating the trajectory run and finishing
with a landing or splash-down.

The teacher's own notes

Theme 5 Props

5.1 Poles

The dance is based on gestures and positions taken from martial arts.

Resources

1. Enough poles between 1.2 and 1.5 metres in length for the class to work individually, e.g. broom handles, garden canes etc.

2. Music: any slow Chinese or Japanese music will act as background and give atmosphere.

Exploring the ideas

☐1 Keeping two hands in contact with the pole throughout, familiarise yourself with ways in which the pole can be manipulated.

☐2 Find stances which suggest a threatening posture and try stepping into them.

Teaching point
Pupils should be aware of the design the body makes with the pole.

☐3 In twos, using the words **approach – circle – retreat from** your partner, work out possibilities.

Teaching points
(a) SAFETY: The movements are performed in a deliberate way, suggesting caution and respect for the opponent.

(b) Alternatives are to match the position of the poles or contrast them (i.e. one vertical, one horizontal). Poles can be kept in contact with the partner's, dancers holding a threatening stance and then circling.

(c) Focus on their partner.

Making the dance

Taking any or all of your ideas, make a partner dance.

Teaching point
Encourage pupils to use a variety of levels; this may bring in jumping and kneeling.

Threatening posture

42

Sharing the work

All duos are performed a few at a time.
The remaining pupils observe.

Teaching point
Pupils' observation is directed towards dances
which have interesting spatial designs.

Possible developments

Depending on the pole used, try using it to
support weight in balances and jumps.

SAFETY: Check that the floor surface and
poles are such that this can be done safely.

The teacher's own notes

5.2 Masks

This unit explores the way in which the identity is hidden or transformed by a mask and another can be adopted.

Resources

A range of masks, those made from unusual objects such as rubber gloves, lampshade sections etc. may give rise to more original ideas than manufactured ones.

Exploring the ideas

The masks can be supplied or made in advance by the pupils.

Study your mask and then wear it. Find three still positions, or poses, which would be appropriate for your character. Move from one to the other so that you begin to travel to a different part of the room.

Teaching point
Dancers should consider changes of level, direction and focus.

Making the dance

In fives, agree a meeting point in the room. Each person uses their travel-into-still position sequence to arrive there. The group arranges itself as if for a group photo, making the masks the most important feature.

Teaching point
The group agrees the front for the dance and ends facing its audience.

Sharing the work

Groups perform one at a time.

Teaching point
The class looks for good use of body design during travelling and in the still positions.

Possible developments

◇ Wearing the mask on the back of the head and adjusting the movements accordingly.

◇ Interaction between two or more of the dancers, e.g. a question and answer dance, where each moves alternately in response to the other.

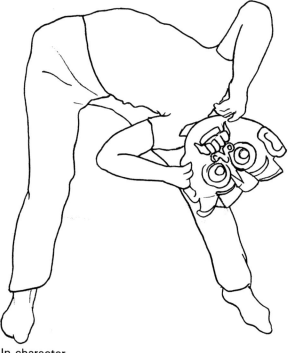

In character

The teacher's own notes

5.3 Fabrics

Ways of moving with material and the ways material moves are the source of ideas for the dance.

Resources

1. Enough large pieces of fabric for one between two, approximately single sheet size. The types of fabric will determine the possibilities.

2. Music: 'Orinocco Flow'. Watermark. WEA WX199C.

Exploring the ideas

Using sheets or large pieces of material, try out the ideas in pairs, of lifting and lowering, travelling with the material, wrapping and uncovering and transporting each other.

Teaching points
(a) Travelling should be done with the fabric high and low.

(b) Timing is an important element.

Sharing the work

All duos are performed.

Teaching points
(a) Observers are asked to look for original and effective ways in which the fabric is used.

(b) Dancers who have incorporated the movement qualities of the fabric into their own movement may also be chosen for comment.

Possible developments

◇ Working in larger groups.

◇ Working with floaty, stretch or transparent fabrics will give different possibilities.

Making the dance

Using your ideas, plan and practise a duo dance in which at least one of you remains in contact with the fabric and in which the material plays an important part.

Teaching point
Remind the class to keep the fabric on the move, if possible.

Moving with material

The teacher's own notes

5.4 Hats

A humorous dance in which the hat determines the character.

Resources

1. A large variety of hats.

2. 'Perk's Theme'. *The Railway Children* soundtrack (LP). SCX 6446. 'Overture'. *Captain Beaky and his Band* (LP). Polydor 2383 46Z.

Exploring the ideas

1 Who might wear the hat you have chosen? Put on the hat and try to take on the character at the same time!

Teaching point
The posture or the way in which the spine is bent, stretched or twisted will help to create the character.

2 Find three or four clear gestures that would fit the person.

Teaching point
Remind the class to make sure that gestures are clear and exaggerated to the point of humour. This may mean making some of them very small and precise as well as the more obvious large ones. Gestures may use the clothing being worn (e.g. brushing off dust specks, re-adjusting clothing) or they may be to do with the way of life (e.g. model strikes a pose).

3 Try walking as your character might.

Teaching points
(a) Pupils will need to consider the situation your character might find themselves in, e.g. old lady going shopping.

(b) It may help pupils to think of words which would be appropriate, e.g. patrol, shuffle, totter.

Making the dance

① Choreograph the sequence of gestures to a set number of beats, given by the teacher (i.e. 16) and then repeat this.

② Double the number of beats (i.e. 32) is then used to perform any combinations of the travelling actions and the gestures already practised may be incorporated. The dance finishes with a still position.

Posing in character

Teaching point
By keeping the dance within a prescribed number of beats, pupils are challenged to make decisions about how best to show the character in the dance in a limited amount of time.

Sharing the work

All solos are performed.

Teaching point
Comments are invited on dancers who have captured a humorous element in their work.

Possible developments

◇1 Interaction in twos or more to make a partner or small-group dance.

◇2 Use of additional props, e.g. chair, walking-stick etc.

◇3 Teacher gives the setting in which the character finds him/herself. The character then interacts with that situation.

5.5 Chairs

The interplay of three dancers is the focus, with the added dimension of having to use two chairs in a prescribed way.

Resources

1. Prepared music, *see Exploring The Ideas* ② (teaching point a).

2. Sketches from the TV programme *Whose line is it anyway?*

Exploring the ideas

The purpose of the dance is to develop pupils' ability to act spontaneously whilst working with others.

① Each trio has two chairs. Interact with each other through dance; but at all times one person must be sitting, another in contact with the second chair whilst the third may not be in contact with either. How and when you move is for you to improvise.

Teaching points
(a) Pupils need to be aware of each other, so that if one leaves a chair, another immediately uses it. Partners should give each other movement cues to what they are about to do.

(b) In order to develop this as improvisation, it is important that pupils do not discuss at this stage.

(c) The task may be interpreted more broadly, e.g. take weight on the chair, rather than sit, the chairs may be moved, or placed in unconventional positions.

② The above process is repeated, but this time to music.

Teaching points
(a) Four short extracts of contrasting music are used, each 20–30 seconds long and including examples such as opera, reggae, marching bands and love songs.

(b) Movements should be made to fit the mood and style of each piece of music.

Making the dance

From the improvised ideas, the group selects, plans and practises their dance.

Teaching point
Innovative interpretations of the task should be encouraged.

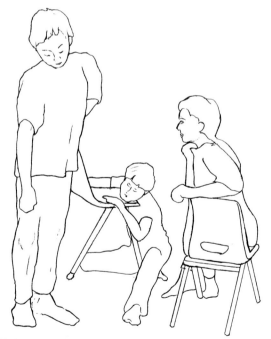

Sitting, leaning, standing

Sharing the work

Two or three trios perform at a time.

Teaching point
Observers are asked to look for surprises in ways the task has been interpreted.

Possible developments

A larger number of extracts of music.

The teacher's own notes

Theme 6 North American Indians

6.1 Stalking

This module introduces pupils to a very different culture from their own, one which is dwindling and which makes demands on their imaginations. In this unit, a variety of actions are used to represent the task of stalking, once a skill essential to survival.

Resources

1. Information about different North American tribes, their names, habitat, customs, etc.

2. Music: Various tracks from *Spirit of the Redman*. New World NWC 601. 'The Snake' and other tracks from *Medicine Dance*. New World NWC 217.

Exploring the ideas

[1] Introduce the idea of North American Indians and stalking.

[2] Discuss the possible ways of travelling when stalking, e.g. crawling, tip-toeing, shadowing, running lightly.

[3] Try out these ideas.

Teaching point
Focus is important, keep eyes on the target throughout.

Making the dance

① Select various ways of following your pathway, showing transitions of levels and speeds.

Teaching points
(a) Encourage awareness of good spacing.

(b) Remembering the pathway accurately is important.

(c) Retracing part of the pathway may be included.

(d) It is important that this is performed quietly and with concentration, or the hunter could become the hunted if you draw attention to yourself.

② The stalking includes pauses when the hunter freezes, and surveys the scene.

Stalking

Teaching point
Encourage dancers to hold still: the image is of the hunter being in danger of being spotted. The looking action can be extended by asking pupils to look around by moving their eyes only, then by moving their heads and then by 'looking' with the whole body.

Sharing the work

Half-class groups demonstrate.

Teaching point
The qualities to look for are concentration, quiet controlled movement and variety of ideas.

Possible developments

The best movement ideas can be singled out, and the rest of the class learns them.

6.2 The Flight of the Arrow

This dance takes as its starting point the actions of drawing a bow, the flight of the arrow and its impact.

Resources

As for *Stalking* (page 52).

Exploring the ideas

The dance consists of three actions (preparation, action and recovery) which may be developed and taught by the teacher *or* generated during experimental work by the pupils and selected by the teacher. The whole class learns all three actions. The teacher will determine the movement, the direction, the group formations, use of unison or canon, etc.

1 *Drawing the bow* – A circular throwing action puts the bow and the body abruptly and powerfully into position (preparation). Pulling back the bow involves a slow gathering of tension, the largest possible movement, including a transfer of weight backwards (action).

2 *The path of the arrow* – Releasing the arrow could be shown through a travelling jump with the body extended in the direction of flight. The movement could be finished with a rolling action or sinking into the ground to finish still.

Making the dance

The class is divided into four groups, each working on the diagonal, from one corner of the room. Each group performs in turn the action of pulling the bow and following the path towards the middle of the room, before retreating slowly back into position as the next group takes over. This order is repeated and then a simple unison movement (for example) rising and turning may be added to finish the dance.

Teaching points
(a) Groups will need to be aware of timing and spacing.
(b) Stillness must be maintained when other groups are moving.

Drawing the bow

Sharing the work

Half of each group demonstrations.

Teaching point
Points to look for are groups who are working in unison and individuals who are carrying out the action effectively.

Possible developments

More complex movement can be chosen, the dance lengthened by changing the order, formations, etc. – for example, lines that work through each other.

The teacher's own notes

6.3 Choreographing from 'The Flight of the Arrow'

Pupils take the elements of the set dance and use them, concentrating on composition to develop their own small group dances.

Resources

As for *Stalking* (page 52).

Exploring the ideas

Basing your ideas upon the set motif, experiment with ways of developing it by changing the order, varying timing, levels, directions and introducing turning, jumping and travelling.

Teaching points
(a) Pupils should be encouraged to experiment freely and try to make the movement their own.

(b) The movement can be transferred to the other side of the body.

Making the dance

In threes, share your ideas and compose a short dance using these.

Teaching points
(a) Pupils should all contribute to the process.
(b) Variety and contrast should determine the variations chosen.

Sharing the work

Trios demonstrate in groups.

Teaching point
Observers should look for and select for comment interpretations which are original and appropriate (i.e. the bow image is still retained).

Possible developments

◇ The trio could be asked to use unison and canon as in the set dance.

◇ Two groups work together, learning each others' dance and adding one onto the other.

Choreographing from 'Flight of the Arrow'

The teacher's own notes

6.4 Weaving

Another important skill was that of weaving; here the dance explores this as a stimulus for making another dance.

Resources

As for *Stalking* (page 52).

Exploring the ideas

1 Look at examples of weaving (material, basket work, etc.) and the ideas of moving in and out, over, under and round pointed out.

2 Form circles in groups of 8, facing alternate ways. Teach a chain figure, everyone moves round the circle in the direction they are facing, passing the first person with right shoulders, the second with their left and so on until they return to their original place.

Teaching point
If pupils find it difficult, try by offering right hand to the first person met, left to the second person etc.

3 In eights, join hands in a line, experimenting with ways of moving in and out of each other by passing between each other, under the linked arms, without breaking contact. The movements must be slow enough for the group to resolve itself into a straight line again.

Teaching points
(a) Choose leaders who will work with control and be aware of their groups in the first instance.

(b) Other pupils should then have the opportunity to lead.

(c) The group will eventually decide who is the best leader. Quality of work will be improved if pupils work with as much space between them as possible, so that the intricacies of the group shapes can be observed.

4 Once 3 has been successfully experienced, groups can cross between each other by stepping over the linked arms.

Dancing a chain figure

Making the dance

As a group, choose three or four from your range of ideas, using some with and some without contact, over and/or under patterns. Each pattern begins and ends with the line spread to its full extent.

Teaching point
All members should contribute to the process of remembering the dance order.

Sharing the work

Each group of eight performs independently.

Teaching point:
Sensitive leadership and co-operation within the group are the important features to note.

Possible developments

◇ Larger groups.

◇ The line can be led from both ends simultaneously, this can lead to symmetrical formations and also be used to reverse the original circles (i.e. back to centre).

The teacher's own notes

6.5 Ritual Dance

Ritual dances are an important part of the North American Indian's way of life. Pupils develop their own version of a ritual dance.

Resources

As for *Stalking* (page 52).

Exploring the ideas

Class is divided into 6, 9 or 12 groups depending on class size. Groups are assigned to work on one of the three dimensions, i.e. up and down, side to side or forwards and backwards.

By yourself, explore circular actions which move in these directions, including gestures and travelling.

Teaching point
Emphasise that the movements should eventually be performed with a sense of ritual, i.e. with dignity and purpose.

Making the dance

① Demonstrate your ideas to the group, which then selects a series to be combined into the final dance.

② Decide as a group on the focus and orientation of the dance and practise the performance.

Teaching point
Encourage groups to choose a mixture of gesture and travelling, and to recognise the importance of held positions.

Sharing the work

Three groups at a time, one working on each dimension, to demonstrate.

Teaching points
(a) Ask the class to look for the group that has used gesture, travelling and particularly stillness.

(b) Also, can they see which groups have conveyed a sense of ritual?

Ritual

Possible developments

The three demonstration groups can be 'orchestrated' by the observers, i.e. their relationships changed spatially, the timing of the starts altered so that the three combine into a final dance.

The teacher's own notes